THEORY TEST COMPANION

London: The Stationery Office

Contents

Introduction

Do I take my theory test before I sign up for driving lessons?

No, not at all, in fact you should be having driving lessons as you're studying for the theory test. This will allow you to put what you're learning into practice on the road. It's important that you know about safety and regulations whilst you're learning to drive.

Your test certificate only lasts for two years. If you don't pass your practical test within this time you'll have to start again.

How do I find an instructor?

Choose an Approved Driving Instructor (ADI), as they will have reached a standard set by the Driving Standards Agency (DSA). They're graded 1-6, 4 being the standard, 5 and 6 reaching a higher standard of instruction. Make enquiries about this before you make a decision. Ask your friends about their instructor, but choose someone you're comfortable with. You can always change your instructor if this isn't the case.

Why do I need this book?

You'll be asked 35 questions during your on-screen test. You'll have to get at least 30 correct before you get a pass certificate and you'll need that before you can book a driving test. It's important you're well prepared or else you could be wasting money by having to take the test more than once. Anyway, being well prepared should make you safer on the road which could mean that you'll pass your driving test sooner.

How to use this book

The test covers various subjects and all of them are covered in this book. You'll notice that they're colour coded for easy reference. The questions you'll be asked are based on these, so if you study this book you won't find the test difficult at all.

Questions in the test are based on information taken from the three books listed below.

Icon references in the margin let you refer to the original text. This gives you information in more detail.

 rule/page no. in *The Highway Code*

 page no. in *Driving: The Essential Skills*

 page no. in *Know Your Traffic Signs*

We have provided you with a question paper on page 95 so that you can practice. You can also buy the *Official Theory Test for Car Drivers* which shows you all the questions, together with the answers and a brief explanation.

1 Alertness

*"DRIVING SAFELY TAKES A LOT OF CONCENTRATION.
LOOK AROUND CONSTANTLY AND BE ALERT"*

Observation

Driving safely takes a lot of concentration. Look around constantly and assess the changing situations as you drive.

Be aware of traffic all around you. Before you carry out any manoeuvre you should

- use your mirrors
- look around for a final check
- signal if necessary.

Be particularly careful before you overtake. Ensure that

- you have a clear view of the road ahead – there shouldn't be any bends or dips
- you have enough time to complete the manoeuvre safely.

It's also important for other road users to know you're there.
- When it starts to get dark, switch on your lights, even if the street lights aren't on.

- Where you can't be seen, such as at a hump-
  back bridge, consider using your horn.

Anticipation and awareness

Look at the road signs and markings; these give
you information about any hazards. You should
- follow their advice
- slow down if necessary.

Watch other road users. Try to anticipate their
actions so you're ready if you need to slow
down or change direction.

Be aware of other, more vulnerable road users.
Watch out for
- pedestrians, especially where they may be
  hidden or approaching a crossing
- cyclists, always pass slowly and leave plenty
  of room.

If you're approaching traffic lights that have
been green for some time, be prepared to stop
because they may change.

However well prepared you are, you may still
have to stop quickly in an emergency. Keep
both hands on the wheel as you brake to keep
control of your vehicle.

Concentration

Always plan your journey so you
- know what route you need to take
- have regular rest stops.

You'll not be able to concentrate properly if
you're tired. It's particularly easy to feel sleepy
on a motorway, so
- don't drive continuously for more than
  two hours

- ensure you've a supply of fresh air
- if you feel tired, leave at the next exit. Find a safe place to stop and have a short nap.

Distraction

Don't let passengers distract you. If you argue with them it will take your mind off driving. Loud music and high spirits may mean you're having fun, but it can be distracting for the driver, and could end in disaster.

You can also be distracted by
- objects hanging in the car
- tuning your radio or inserting a cassette
- looking at a map.

Just taking your eyes off the road for a second could be disastrous. In that second, at 60 mph, your car will travel 27 metres.

"PEOPLE WHO RING YOU ON A MOBILE PHONE MAY NOT HAVE YOUR ROAD SAFETY AS A HIGH PRIORITY"

Using a mobile phone while you're driving is extremely dangerous. No phone call is that important. Be safe, switch it off and use the mail retrieval service. Wait until you're parked in a safe and proper place before you
- retrieve any messages
- make any calls.

Is it OK to use a 'hands-free' phone when driving?

Just because it's hands-free doesn't make it safe, it can still distract you. The person you're talking to can't see the traffic situation. They won't stop speaking to you if you're approaching a hazard.

It's safer not to use a phone at all if you're driving. Wait and find a safe place to stop.

I've seen yellow lines painted at intervals across the road. What do they mean?

These encourage drivers to reduce their speed. They may be red. You often see them on approach to a

- hazard (such as a roundabout)
- reduced speed limit.

I have heard the term 'blind spot'. What does this mean?

Blind spots are areas that can't be seen either when using normal forward vision or when using the mirrors.

Be aware that a lorry driver can't see you if you're close behind. Keep well back so the driver can see you.

"EXTERIOR MIRRORS WILL HELP REDUCE BLIND SPOTS"

2 Attitude

Safe driving is all about developing the correct attitude and approach together with a sound knowledge of driving techniques.

However good, fast or expensive your vehicle, it's you, the driver, who determines how safe it is.

Consideration

Be considerate to other road users. Other types of vehicle, cyclists and horse riders have just as much right to use the road as you.

Horses become frightened easily and the rider could lose control. When passing them
* keep your speed right down
* give them plenty of room.

Take care if there are animals, such as sheep, on the road. Stop and switch off your engine if necessary or if you're asked to do so.

If you're driving a slow-moving vehicle, consider the other drivers behind you. If there's a long queue

• pull over as soon as you can do so safely
• let the traffic pass.

Try to be considerate. Think how you would feel if you were one of the following drivers. They may not be as patient as you.

Help other road users by signalling correctly and taking up the correct position at junctions. For instance, if you want to turn right, get into the right hand lane. A badly positioned vehicle could prevent following vehicles proceeding.

Following safely

Keep a safe distance from the vehicle in front
• in good, dry conditions leave a
  two-second gap
• in wet weather leave four seconds.

Tailgating – driving too close to the vehicle in front – is
• very dangerous
• intimidating for the driver in front.

Keep well back, especially from a large vehicle. You'll be able to see further down the road and therefore be prepared for any hazards.

If the driver behind is following too closely, gradually increase the gap between you and the vehicle in front. This will give you a greater safety margin.

If another driver cuts in front of you, drop back to maintain your correct separation distance.

Courtesy

Be patient with other road users. Be aware that not everyone obeys the rules. Try to be calm and tolerant, however difficult it seems. For instance, if a vehicle pulls out in front of you at a junction, slow down, don't get annoyed with them.

Only sound your horn if there's danger and you need to let others know you're there. Don't sound it through impatience.

"BE COURTEOUS AND DIP YOUR LIGHTS AT NIGHT TO AVOID DAZZLING OTHER DRIVERS"

At night, don't dazzle other drivers. Dip your
lights when you're
• following another vehicle
• meeting another vehicle.

If you're queuing in traffic at night, use your
handbrake. Keeping your foot on the brake
could dazzle the vehicles behind you.

Priority

Give priority to emergency vehicles. It's
important for them to proceed quickly through
traffic. Someone's life might depend on it. Pull
over to let them through as soon as you can do
so safely.

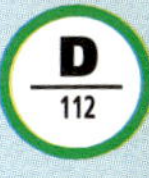

As well as the normal fire, police and
ambulance, the following services may use a
blue flashing light:
• coastguard
• bomb disposal
• mountain rescue
• blood transfusion.
Doctors may use green flashing lights.

Give priority to buses pulling out from bus
stops, as long as you can do so safely. In some
areas, bus lanes allow buses to proceed quickly
through traffic. Be aware of road signs and
markings so you don't use bus lanes while
they're in operation.

Watch out for pedestrians at or approaching a
zebra crossing:
• be prepared to slow down and stop
• be patient if they're a bit slow
• don't encourage them to cross by waving or
  flashing your headlights – there may be
  another vehicle coming.

If you're approaching a pelican crossing and the amber light is flashing
• give way to pedestrians on the crossing
• don't move off until the crossing is clear.

Treat a pelican crossing as one complete crossing if it crosses the road in a straight line, even if it has a central island. If there's a pedestrian from the other side still crossing when the amber light is showing, you must wait.

Puffin crossings are electronically controlled. Sensors mean the red light stays on until the person has reached a safe position. There's no flashing amber phase – the sequence follows normal traffic lights.

Toucan crossings allow cyclists to cross at the same time as pedestrians.

FAQs

*I've seen this sign –
what does it mean?*
This sign applies to trams only. Even if
there aren't any trams where you live,
you still need to know how to deal with
them in case you ever visit a town with them.

Give cyclists extra room where there are tram
rails. The slippery rails may be difficult for them
to negotiate.

Why do large vehicles 'hog' the road?
Larger vehicles need more room to manoeuvre.
This will affect their position when approaching
junctions, especially when turning left. Keep
well back and don't try to pass them on the left
as the rear of the vehicle will cut in.

A large vehicle is trying to overtake me, but is taking a long time, what should I do?
Slow down and let them pass. They will need
more time than a car to pass you.

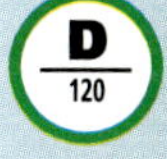

What do I do if I'm travelling at the speed limit and a driver comes up behind flashing their headlights or trying to overtake?
Keep a steady course and allow them to
overtake. Don't try to stop them, they could
become more frustrated.

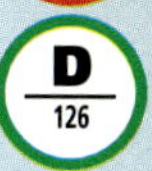

I'm never too sure when I should flash my headlights.
Only flash your headlights to show other
road users you're there. It's not a signal to
show priority.

3 Safety and your vehicle

Look after your car and it will look after you by being more economical and lasting longer. Remember that a clean engine is kinder to the environment.

"A CLEAN ENGINE IS KINDER TO THE ENVIRONMENT"

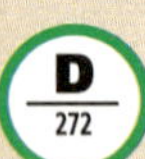

Basic maintenance

Regular care should ensure that your car is safe. Check

- lights, brakes, steering, exhaust system, seat belts, horn, speedometer, wipers and washers. These must all be working properly
- oil and water levels. This is especially important before a long journey
- brake fluid. If this is allowed to get low it's dangerous and could cause an accident
- the windscreen. This must be in good condition
- tyre pressures. Do this regularly, at least once a week. Check when they are cold to get a more accurate reading. Under-inflated tyres can affect

14

– steering – it will feel heavy

– fuel consumption – it may increase

– braking

- tyre condition. The tread must be at least 1.6 mm deep across the centre three-quarters of the breadth of the tyre and around the entire outer circumference. It's illegal to drive with tyres that have deep cuts in the side walls.

Uneven wear on the tyres can be caused by faults in the

- braking system
- suspension
- wheel alignment.

If the wheels are unbalanced they could cause the steering to vibrate.

Defects

If you've a basic understanding of how your car works it'll help you recognise the signs of a defect. It's important that your car's checked regularly by a qualified mechanic, especially the brakes and the steering.

Warning lights on the dashboard monitor the performance of the engine and give you warning of any defects.

- Check your vehicle handbook for their meaning.
- Don't ignore the warning – it could affect your safety.

The ABS warning light should go out when the vehicle's travelling at 5-10 mph. If it doesn't, have it checked by a qualified mechanic.

To check the condition of the shock absorbers,

'bounce' the vehicle. Push down hard on each corner and it shouldn't continue to bounce unduly when released.

Consult a garage as soon as possible if
- the steering vibrates – the wheels may need balancing
- the vehicle pulls to one side when you brake – your brakes may need adjusting.

Safety equipment

Modern cars are fitted with equipment designed with your safety in mind.

Wear your seat belt and make sure your passengers wear theirs (unless exempt). You, as a driver, are responsible for making sure that children under 14 wear a suitable restraint. Never fit a rear-facing baby seat in a seat protected by an airbag. This could cause fatal injuries.

When you get into the car

- adjust the seat to ensure you can reach all the controls in comfort

- adjust the head restraint to help prevent neck injury in a collision

- wear suitable shoes so that you can keep control of the pedals
- adjust the mirrors to maximise your field of vision. Convex mirrors give a wider view but can make vehicles look further away than they are. If you're reversing and can't see behind you, get someone to guide you.

If visibility's poor, use dipped headlights. It's important for other road users to see you. If there's thick fog, use your fog lights.

Hazard warning lights are fitted so you can warn drivers of a hazard ahead, such as

- when you've broken down
- queuing traffic on a dual carriageway or motorway.

Don't use them as an excuse to park illegally, even for a short time.

Security

Make it as difficult as you can for a thief to either break into your car or steal it:

- remove the keys and lock your car even if you're only leaving it for a short time
- put any contents, especially valuables, out of sight, or better still take them with you
- don't leave the vehicle registration documents in the car. The thief could declare ownership
- at night, park in a well-lit area. Dark areas in car parks are high risk.

To make it more difficult for the opportunist thief you can
- fit an anti-theft alarm or immobiliser
- use a visible security device such as a steering wheel or handbrake lock
- have the vehicle registration number etched on the windows.

"YOU CAN FIT A VARIETY OF SECURITY DEVICES TO YOUR VEHICLE"

Radios and other forms of in-car entertainment are prime targets for thieves. If you can, install a security coded radio. This is of little use once it's stolen.

"CONSIDER JOINING A VEHICLE WATCH SCHEME IF THERE'S ONE IN YOUR AREA"

Consider joining a vehicle watch scheme if there's one in your area.

Environment

Motor vehicles can harm the environment, resulting in

- air pollution
- damage to buildings
- using up of natural resources.

Help the environment by reducing your emissions and improving your fuel consumption at the same time:

- reduce your speed. Your car will use 30% more fuel if driven at 70 mph instead of 50 mph.
- plan well ahead so you don't have to accelerate and brake harshly
- have your vehicle serviced and tuned properly
- make sure your tyres are correctly inflated.

Don't

- carry unnecessary weight or leave an empty roof rack on your car
- over-rev in lower gears.

Try not to use your car to make a lot of short journeys, think about walking or cycling instead. Using public transport or sharing a car can reduce the volume of traffic and the emissions it creates.

Modern trams use electric power. They reduce traffic and noise pollution.

"MODERN TRAMS USE ELECTRIC POWER
AND REDUCE TRAFFIC"

Make sure your filler cap is securely fastened. If it's loose, it could spill fuel which

- wastes fuel unnecessarily
- makes the road slippery for other road users.

"ENSURE THAT YOU TAKE YOUR CAR FOR REGULAR SERVICES"

Having your car serviced regularly will give better fuel economy and your exhaust emissions will be cleaner. Your vehicle will have to pass an emissions test as part of the MOT test.

If you service your own vehicle, dispose of old engine oil and batteries responsibly. Take them to an authorised site or a garage. Don't pour oil down the drain.

Also bear in mind noise pollution. In built-up areas don't use your car horn between 11.30 pm and 7.00 am, unless another vehicle poses a danger.

FAQs
I have heard the term 'dry steering' – what does this mean?
This is when you turn the steering wheel while the car isn't moving. It can cause unnecessary wear to the tyres and steering mechanism.

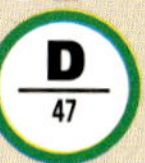

What is a catalytic converter?

A catalytic converter is fitted to the exhaust and reduces emissions. It acts like a filter, removing some of the toxic waste.

"A 'CATOLIT' CONVERTER..."

Road humps have been installed in our area. What other types of traffic calming are there?

As well as road humps, road narrowing and chicanes may be used. These are used to slow the traffic down, so keep your speed down throughout the area.

A reduced speed limit of 20 mph is being introduced into many narrow residential streets.

"THERE ARE VARIOUS TYPES OF TRAFFIC CALMING SCHEMES"

Look out for the signs, and remember the measures are there for a good reason; they could save lives.

In an automatic car, what is 'kick down'?
This is a device that gives quick acceleration when needed, for example, to overtake. Excessive use of this will burn more fuel.

On a trip to London I saw red lines on the side of the road. What are they for?
These indicate 'red routes'. They help the traffic flow by restricting stopping on these routes.

I've heard of 'brake fade'. What does it mean?
This is when the brakes become less effective because of overheating. It may happen if they're used continuously, such as on a long, steep downhill stretch of road. Using a lower gear will help braking.

4 Safety margins

It's essential that you always keep in mind the safety of not only yourself, but your passengers and other road users as well.

Reduce your chances of having an accident by knowing safety margins and the risk of not adhering to them. Never take unnecessary risks.

Keep control of your car by using the correct procedures. For instance, when you're travelling downhill, control your speed by
• selecting a lower gear
• braking gently.

Don't 'coast' (i.e. travel in neutral or with the clutch pressed down) as this reduces your control.

"COASTING IS DANGEROUS AS IT REDUCES YOUR CONTROL"

Stopping distance

Leave enough room between you and the car in front so you can pull up safely if it slows down or stops suddenly. Your overall stopping distance is the distance your car travels
- from the moment you realise you must brake
- to the moment the vehicle stops.

This is made up of **thinking** distance and **braking** distance.

Study the typical thinking, braking and stopping distances given in *The Highway Code*. The figures given are the stopping distances if you're travelling in a vehicle with good tyres and brakes
- on a dry road
- in good conditions.

Don't just learn the figures – you need to be able to judge the distance. A useful method is to leave a two-second time gap between yourself and the vehicle in front.

In other conditions you need to increase these distances:
- when it's raining or the road is wet – double the distance
- when it's icy – ten times the distance.

Weather conditions

Weather conditions have a great effect on your safety margins. If the weather's really bad, such as snow, ice or thick fog, consider whether your journey's really necessary. Never underestimate the dangers.

Before starting a journey in freezing weather, clear ice and snow from your windows, lights, mirrors and number plates. When driving

- use the highest gear you can
- brake gently and in plenty of time
- be prepared to stop and clean your windscreen by hand if the wipers aren't effective.

When it's foggy

- allow more time for your journey
- slow down as your visibility is reduced
- use dipped headlights even in daylight. If visibility falls below 100 metres (328 feet) use fog lights if you've them. Remember to switch them off when the fog lifts.

Aquaplaning may happen in heavy rain. The tyres lift off the road surface and skate on a film of water. The steering becomes light.

- Ease off the accelerator.
- Don't brake until your steering feels normal again.

"AQUAPLANING CAN OCCUR WHEN THE TYRES LIFT FROM THE ROAD SURFACE ON A FILM OF WATER"

If you've driven through deep water such as a ford or a flood, test your brakes. If necessary, dry them out by pressing lightly on the brake pedal as you go along.

Hot weather can also pose a danger. The road surface could become soft and your tyres might not grip so well. This may affect your
- braking
- steering.

Bright sunlight can dazzle. Other drivers might not be able to see your indicators blinking if they are dazzled. Consider giving a hand signal as well.

High winds can blow you off course especially on an open stretch of road. They have an even greater effect on high-sided vehicles and cyclists. Take care if you pass a cyclist as they may be blown off course by a sudden gust.

"BEWARE OF HIGH WINDS:
CYCLISTS MAY BE BLOWN OFF
COURSE BY A SUDDEN GUST"

Skidding

Skidding is mainly caused by the driver. Drivers need to adjust their driving to the road, weather and traffic conditions.

There's most risk of skidding in wet or icy conditions. Black ice isn't obvious until you feel the steering becoming light. Be aware that in very cold weather it could be a hazard.

Reduce the risk of skidding and wheelspin by driving
- at a low speed
- in as high a gear as possible.

Scan the road ahead for clues such as road signs and markings. You shouldn't then be taken by surprise. You can

- slow down gradually before you reach the hazard, such as a bend
- avoid sudden steering movements.

If you do start skidding

- release the footbrake and reapply it gently
- steer smoothly in the direction of the skid – if the back of the car skids to the right, steer carefully to the right, and vice versa.

Anti-lock braking systems (ABS) reduce the risk of skidding when braking in an emergency. Wheel speed sensors anticipate when a wheel is about to lock. If you're driving a vehicle with ABS

- apply the footbrake rapidly and firmly
- don't release the brake pedal until you have stopped.

ABS doesn't necessarily reduce your stopping distance but you can continue to steer while braking because the wheels are prevented from locking. It may not work as effectively where there's

- surface water
- loose road surfaces.

FAQs

Why does my instructor tell me to keep well to the left before a right-hand bend?

Keeping well to the left improves your view of the road ahead and gives you an earlier indication of any hazards.

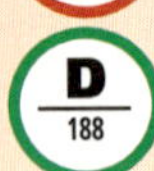

How can I park my car safely on a downhill slope?

Apply the handbrake firmly and turn the steering wheel towards the kerb. This will help stop your vehicle rolling downhill.

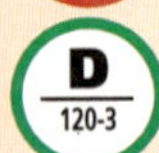

I know overtaking is a dangerous manoeuvre – are there any places that I definitely need to avoid?

Always ensure you've enough time to complete the manoeuvre safely. In particular don't overtake

- *where your view ahead is blocked (e.g. by a bend)*
- *when approaching a junction*
- *if you're intending to turn off the road shortly afterwards.*

"WHEN OVERTAKING, ALWAYS ENSURE YOU'VE ENOUGH TIME TO COMPLETE THE MANOEUVRE SAFETY"

What are the benefits of a four-wheel drive vehicle?

It has improved road holding. The extra grip helps when travelling on slippery or uneven roads.

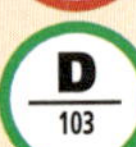

Why are there so many speed humps around?

These traffic calming measures are normally found in built-up areas to improve the safety of the area. Slow right down as you approach and drive over them.

5 Hazard awareness

When you start to learn to drive you'll be concentrating on the basic controls of the car. As your skill improves so will your ability to recognise hazards on the road.

A hazard is a situation which may require you as a driver to respond by taking action such as braking or steering. These can be

- static hazards – such as roundabouts and junctions
- moving hazards – other road users
- road and weather conditions.

Static hazards

There are numerous types of static hazard; bends, junctions, roundabouts, parked

vehicles, roadworks, traffic calming, crossings, traffic lights.

All of these may require you to respond in some way, so
• take a mental note of their existence
• slow down and get ready to stop if necessary.

Road signs and markings are there to give you clues. Learn their meanings. Watch out for them so that you can reduce your speed in good time and prepare yourself for any action you may need to take. The same applies to traffic lights, other light signals and signals from police officers.

If you see a sign for a bend ask yourself, 'What if there was a pedestrian or obstruction just around the bend, could I stop in time? Could I do it safely?'

In busy areas, parked cars can cause a hazard. Watch out for
• children dashing out from between the cars
• car doors opening
• cars moving away.

Would you be able to stop?

There's often reduced visibility at junctions, especially in built-up areas. Take extra care and pull forward slowly until you can see down the road.

Don't block a junction, leave it clear to allow vehicles to enter and emerge.

Where lanes are closed
* be ready for cars cutting in front of you
* keep a safe distance from the vehicle in front.

Moving hazards

These are other types of road user; pedestrians,
cyclists, horse riders, large vehicle drivers,
motorcyclists and other car drivers.

Be aware of cyclists and give them plenty
of room:

* they may wobble or swerve to avoid drains
  or potholes

* at junctions or traffic lights, give them time
  to turn or pull away
* before you turn left, check for cyclists filtering
  on your left.

If you see a bus at a bus stop, think

* people may get off the bus and cross
  the road

* the bus may be about to move off.

Watch out for other vehicles, especially motorcyclists, overtaking and cutting in front of you. If you need to, drop back to retain a safe separation distance.

Elderly drivers may not react very quickly, so be patient with them.

Some vehicles have signs on the back, for example, those with arrows or advising of hazardous chemicals. Learn what they mean.

Yourself

Don't allow yourself to become a hazard on the road. You need to be alert at all times.

Don't drive if you're tired. Plan your journey so that you've enough rest stops: at least one every two hours.

If you feel tired
- pull over at a safe place to rest
- on a motorway, leave at the next exit or services.

Always make sure you've plenty of fresh air in your car.

Your concentration can also be affected by
- using a mobile phone
- loud music
- looking at a map.

If you've had an argument, calm down before starting or continuing your journey.

Never drive if you've been drinking. It's not worth taking a chance. If you're driving, don't drink alcohol. If you've had a drink, go home by public transport. Alcohol

- reduces concentration and coordination
- gives a false sense of confidence
- reduces your judgement of speed
- slows down your reactions.

You must be fit to drive. Certain medicines can make you drowsy; check the label or ask your doctor or pharmacist.

Using illegal drugs is highly dangerous. Never take them before driving. If you've been convicted of driving whilst unfit through drink or drugs, the cost of your insurance will rise considerably.

Your eyesight should be of a safe standard. If you need glasses to drive, wear them every time you drive. Don't wear tinted glasses at night.

You must tell the licensing authority if

- your eyesight deteriorates
- you suffer from an illness which may affect your driving.

"IF YOU NEED GLASSES TO DRIVE, WEAR THEM EVERY TIME YOU DRIVE"

Road and weather conditions

Different types of weather can change a normal stretch of road into a hazard. Rain, ice, fog and even bright sunlight can have an effect on safety. Drive accordingly and be aware of the added dangers.

In wet weather
- double your separation distance to four seconds
- spray may reduce your vision.

FAQs

How do I deal with inconsiderate drivers?

There are occasions when we all make misjudgements or mistakes. Be aware that other drivers might not always follow the rules. Stay calm. Don't shout or make rude gestures, this won't help the situation at all.
- *Wait if necessary to allow the other driver to move out of the way.*
- *If you feel upset, stop and take a break if you can.*

Good anticipation skills can help to prevent these incidents becoming accidents.

What restrictions are there on provisional licence holders?

You must not drive
- on your own
- on a motorway.

Are there any moving picture questions in the theory test?

Not at the moment. However there are plans to introduce a hazard perception test as part of the theory test. This will consist of a series of video clips and there'll be training material available to help prepare for the test. In the meantime go to **www.ask-what-if.com** where you'll find details of a hazard awareness video and booklet which is already available.

How do you prevent the car behind driving too closely?

Move over and let the car through if you can. If there's no room and the driver behind seems to be 'pushing' you, increase your distance from the car in front. This will lessen the risk of an accident involving several vehicles.

What do I do if I take the wrong route and find myself in a one-way street?

Don't try to turn round in a one-way street. Continue to the end of the road and then find a safe place to turn round.

What do I do if it looks like the driver in front has forgotten to cancel their right indicator?

Be cautious. Stay behind and don't overtake – they may be unsure of the position of a junction and turn suddenly.

"IF THE DRIVER IN FRONT HAS FORGOTTEN TO CANCEL THEIR RIGHT INDICATOR, BE CAUTIOUS, STAY BEHIND AND DON'T OVERTAKE"

6 Vulnerable road users

The most vulnerable road users are pedestrians, cyclists, motorcyclists and horse riders. Always be aware of their presence and treat them with respect. It's particularly important to show consideration to children, elderly and disabled people.

Learners, inexperienced and older drivers are the most vulnerable types of driver.

Pedestrians

Pedestrians normally use a pavement or footpath. Take extra care if they have to walk in the road

- when the pavement is closed due to street repairs
- on country roads where there's no pavement.

On country roads, pedestrians are advised to walk on the right-hand side of the road so they are facing oncoming traffic. Signs may warn you of people walking in the road.

A large group of people, such as those on an organised walk, may walk on the left-hand side. At night the person at the rear should carry a bright red light to warn approaching vehicles of their presence.

"WATCH OUT FOR PEDESTRIANS ALREADY CROSSING WHEN YOU'RE TURNING INTO A SIDE ROAD"

Watch out for pedestrians already crossing when you're turning into a side road. They have priority, so wait for them to cross.

Be ready to slow down and stop as you approach a pedestrian crossing.

- Zebra crossings – stop if someone is waiting to cross
- Pelican crossings are light controlled. During the flashing amber phase, give way to pedestrians on the crossing. If the lights change to green while someone is still crossing, be patient and wait until they have finished crossing.
- Puffin crossings have sensors to detect when people are on the crossing. The lights don't change from red until the crossing is clear.
- Toucan crossings – cyclists can cross at the same time as pedestrians. There's no flashing amber phase.

Children

Children cause particular problems because they can be unpredictable.

Drive carefully near schools:
- there may be flashing amber lights under a school warning sign. Reduce your speed until you're clear of the area
- be prepared for a school crossing patrol to stop the traffic by stepping out into the road with a stop sign.

"CHILDREN POSE PARTICULAR PROBLEMS BECAUSE THEY CAN BE UNPREDICTABLE"

Don't wait or park on yellow zigzag lines outside a school. A clear view of the crossing area outside the school is needed by
- drivers on the road
- pedestrians on the pavement.

Buses and coaches carrying schoolchildren show a special sign in the back. This indicates that they may stop frequently and not at normal bus stops.

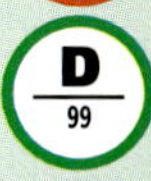

Elderly and disabled pedestrians

If you see elderly people about to cross the road ahead, be careful, as they may have misjudged your speed.

If they are crossing, be patient and allow them to cross in their own time.

Treat disabled pedestrians as you would able-bodied, but be patient as they may need extra time to cross the road.

A person carrying a white stick with a red band is both deaf and blind.

Cyclists

Cyclists should normally follow the same rules as drivers, but they are slower and more vulnerable. In some areas signs may indicate special cycle routes.

If you're overtaking a cyclist, give them as much room as you would a car. They may need to swerve
• to avoid an uneven road surface
• if they're affected by the wind.

A cyclist going slowly, or glancing over their shoulder to check for traffic, may be planning to turn right. Stay behind and give them plenty of room.

Never overtake a cyclist (or moped) just before you turn left. Hold back and wait until they have passed the junction before you turn.

When you're emerging from a junction, look carefully for cyclists. They're not as easy to see as larger vehicles.

Be aware of cyclists at a roundabout. They may decide to stay in the left-hand lane whatever direction they're planning to take. Hold back and give them plenty of room.

Motorcyclists
The points above
• leaving extra room while overtaking
• following behind someone turning right
• emerging from a junction
are also particularly relevant to motorcyclists.

"WHEN YOU'RE MOVING IN QUEUES OF TRAFFIC BE AWARE THAT MOTORCYCLISTS MAY FILTER BETWEEN LANES"

When you're moving in queues of traffic be aware that motorcyclists may
- filter between lanes
- cut in just in front of you
- pass very close to you.

Before you turn right, always check for other traffic, especially motorcyclists, who may be overtaking.

In order to improve their visibility, motorcyclists often wear bright clothing and ride with dipped headlights, even during the day.

Motorcyclists also wear safety equipment, such as a helmet, to protect themselves. If there's been an accident and you find a motorcyclist has been injured, seek medical assistance. Don't remove their helmet unless it's essential to keep them alive.

Animals

Always drive carefully if there are horses or other animals on the road. Go very slowly and be ready to stop. When it's safe to overtake
• drive slowly
• leave plenty of room.

Take particular care when approaching a roundabout. Horse riders, like cyclists, may keep to the left, even if they're signalling right. Stay well back.

Other drivers

The reactions of other drivers, especially inexperienced or older drivers, may be slower than yours. Learner drivers may make a mistake such as stalling at a junction. Try to be patient.

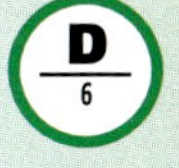

Statistics show that 17 to 25 year olds are the most likely to be involved in a road accident.

Newly qualified drivers can decrease their risk of accidents, particularly on the motorway, by taking further training. Find out more about the Pass Plus scheme from your ADI or by calling 0115 901 2633.

FAQs

Reversing seems to be a dangerous manoeuvre. How can I be sure it's safe?

Always check the area behind the car very carefully. Look especially for children, who are difficult to see. Get out and check if you're not sure. Stop and give way to any pedestrians who are crossing the road behind you.

"LOOK ESPECIALLY FOR CHILDREN, WHO ARE DIFFICULT TO SEE"

What should I do if parked vehicles restrict my view when emerging from a junction?

Stop, then creep forward slowly until you've a clear view.

Apart from where it's illegal, such as yellow lines, are there other places I should avoid when parking?

Don't park where you would cause a danger, such as
- *near the brow of a hill*
- *on the approach to a level crossing*

or where you would cause an obstruction to others, such as

- *at or near a bus stop*
- *in front of a property*
- *where the kerb has been lowered for wheelchairs.*

How can I tell if someone is going to cross the road between parked cars?

You can't, but look for tell-tale signs such as a ball bouncing out onto the road or a bicycle wheel sticking out between cars. Slow down and be prepared to stop.

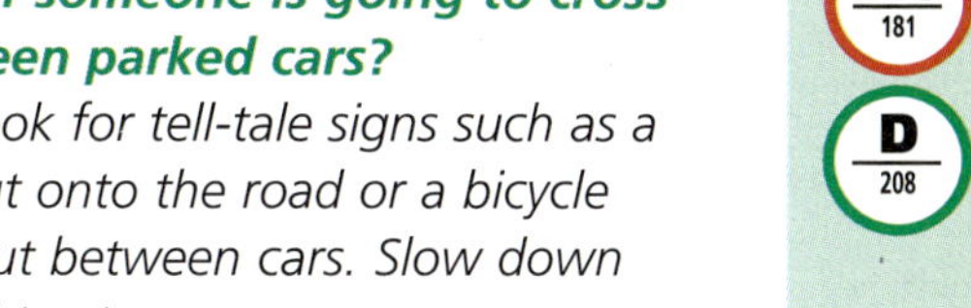

Who is most vulnerable at road junctions?

Junctions are dangerous places, especially for those who can't be seen as easily, e.g. pedestrians, cyclists and motorcyclists. Always take extra care.

What does a flashing amber beacon on the top of a vehicle mean?

This indicates a slow-moving vehicle.

Why do I need to be careful if a bus has stopped on the other side of the road?

Pedestrians may come from behind the bus and cross the road, or dash across from your left.

If I have a collision, what's the first thing I have to do?

Stop. By law, you must stop at the scene of the accident.

A friend wants to teach me to drive. Do they need any special qualifications?

Anyone who accompanies you must

- be over 21
- have held, and still hold, a full licence for that category of vehicle for at least three years.

You're strongly advised to take lessons with an Approved Driving Instructor to ensure that you're taught the correct procedures from the start.

What can I do if I'm being dazzled by the vehicle behind?

Set your mirror to anti-dazzle, if you're able. Slow down and stop if you can't see.

7 Other types of vehicle

You need to take extra care when meeting or following different types of vehicle, both smaller and larger vehicles.

Motorcycles

Motorcyclists are affected more than other vehicles by windy weather. They can be blown sideways and veer into your path more easily, so

- if you're overtaking a motorcyclist allow extra room
- if a motorcyclist in front of you is overtaking a high-sided vehicle, keep well back as they could be blown off course.

Watch out for signs warning you that the road is particularly susceptible to side winds.

Motorcyclists may swerve into the road to avoid uneven or slippery surfaces. Metal drain covers in wet weather are particularly hazardous.

Large vehicles

Large vehicles reduce your view of the road ahead. Keep well back if you're following a large vehicle, especially if you're hoping to overtake. If another car fills the gap you've left, drop back further. This will improve your view of the road ahead.

Overtaking a lorry is more risky because of the length of the vehicle. Never begin to overtake unless you're sure that you can complete the manoeuvre safely.

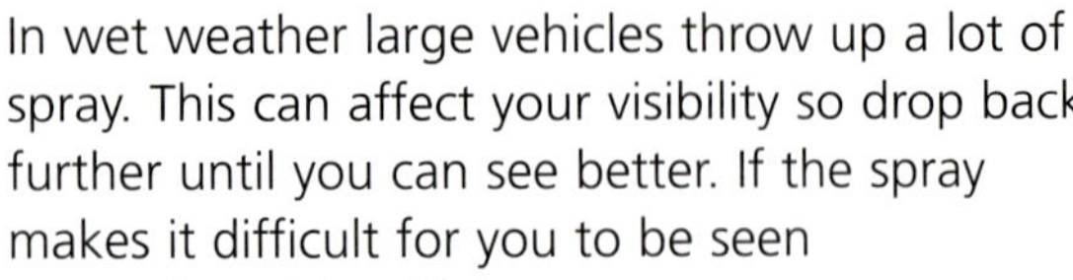

In wet weather large vehicles throw up a lot of spray. This can affect your visibility so drop back further until you can see better. If the spray makes it difficult for you to be seen

- use dipped headlights
- use rear fog lights if visibility is seriously reduced, i.e. less than 100 metres (328 feet).

Stay well back and give lorries plenty of room as they approach or emerge from

- road junctions
- crossroads
- mini-roundabouts.

To get round a corner, they may need to move in the opposite direction to which they're indicating. This is because of the length of their vehicle. If they want to turn left, they may indicate left but move over to the right, and vice versa.

If you're waiting to emerge left from a minor road and a large vehicle is approaching from the right, wait. It may seem as if there's time to turn but the large vehicle could easily hide an overtaking vehicle.

Buses

Bus drivers need to make frequent stops. If a bus pulls up at a bus stop, watch carefully for pedestrians who may get off and cross the road in front of or behind the bus.

Be prepared to give way to a bus which is trying to move off from a bus stop, as long as it's safe to do so.

Trams

Trams operate in some cities. Take extra care – they

- are silent
- move quickly
- can't steer to avoid you.

In these cities, there may be additional white light signals at some traffic lights. These are especially for tram drivers.

FAQs

What kind of rear view mirror should I use if I'm towing a caravan?

It's safest to use extended-arm side mirrors. These help you get a better view behind and around the caravan.

If I'm driving downhill and a lorry coming uphill needs to move out to pass a parked car, should I stop for it?

Slow down and give way if possible. It's much more difficult for large vehicles to stop and then start up again if they are going uphill.

Which vehicles are most affected by crosswinds?

Crosswinds are much more likely to affect cyclists, motorcyclists and high-sided vehicles than they are cars. If you're following or overtaking, be aware that they might swerve suddenly.

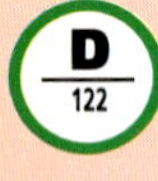

Why are two-way roads divided into three lanes more dangerous?

Traffic in both directions can use the middle lane to overtake, so approaching traffic could be intending to make the same manoeuvre at the same time.

8 Vehicle handling

Various conditions can affect the handling of your vehicle. These can roughly be divided into
- weather and light conditions
- control and speed
- road surfaces.

Weather conditions

Rain or wet conditions

When it's raining or the road is wet, leave at least double the normal stopping distance. If you're following a vehicle at a safe distance and another vehicle pulls into the gap you've left, drop back to regain a safe distance.

If you're driving in very wet weather you may find that your vehicle begins to aquaplane, i.e. slide. This is because water builds up between the tyres and the road and makes the steering feel light.

In winter a ford is more likely to flood, making it difficult to cross. There may be a depth gauge, which will help you decide whether you should go through. If you decide to continue
- use a low gear
- drive through slowly
- test your brakes afterwards: wet brakes are less effective.

Fog

When visibility is seriously reduced you must use headlights, or fog lights if you have them. 'Seriously reduced' generally means if you can't see for more than 100 metres (328 feet).

Never use front or rear fog lights unless visibility is seriously reduced. If you've been using them and conditions improve, remember to switch them off. Don't use fog lights when they're not needed because
- you may be breaking the law
- they can dazzle other drivers
- drivers behind you won't be able to see your brake lights as clearly, or they may think you're braking when you're not.

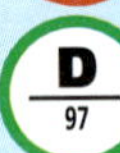

Be especially careful when driving on motorways in fog and always keep your speed down. Reflective studs help you to see the road ahead. In particular
- red studs mark the left-hand edge
- amber studs mark the central reservation.

Very bad weather

If it's very foggy or snow is falling heavily, don't travel unless your journey is essential. If you must travel, take great care and allow plenty of time.

Before you start out, make sure that
- your lights are working
- your windows are clean.

HC
203-10

D
244-51

IF SNOW IS FALLING HEAVILY, DON'T TRAVEL UNLESS YOUR JOURNEY IS ESSENTIAL. IF YOU MUST TRAVEL, TAKE GREAT CARE AND ALLOW PLENTY OF TIME."

In deep snow, consider fitting chains to your wheels to help grip and prevent skidding.

When on the road
- reduce your speed – it's more difficult to see what's happening ahead
- keep well back – increase the gap between yourself and the vehicle ahead in case it stops suddenly. In icy conditions it can take ten times as long to stop compared to dry conditions.

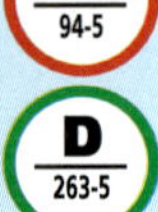

Windy weather

Wind can affect all vehicles. A sudden gust may catch your vehicle

- when passing a high-sided vehicle on the motorway
- when passing bridges, gaps in hedges etc.

Driving at night

Make sure that your headlights don't dazzle

- the vehicle you're following
- any oncoming traffic.

If you're dazzled by the headlights of an oncoming vehicle, slow down or stop to remain in full control.

"IF YOU'RE DAZZLED BY THE HEADLIGHTS OF AN ONCOMING VEHICLE, SLOW DOWN OR STOP TO REMAIN IN FULL CONTROL"

Be extra careful when you overtake at night. You can't see as far ahead and there may be bends in the road.

On a motorway, use
* dipped headlights, even if the road is well lit
* sidelights if you're broken down on the hard shoulder. This will help other road users to see you.

Control and speed

Keep full control of your vehicle at all times. Driving with the clutch down or in neutral for any length of time (coasting) reduces control, especially of steering and braking. This is especially dangerous when travelling downhill as the vehicle will pick up speed quickly and there's no engine braking.

You can use your vehicle's engine to help control your speed. Select a lower gear when driving down a steep hill. This can be especially important as your brakes may become less effective due to overheating.

When driving up a steep hill, the engine will work harder and you'll slow down sooner.

On a single-track road
* take extra care
* keep your speed down, especially at bends
* pull into, or opposite, a passing place if you see a vehicle coming towards you.

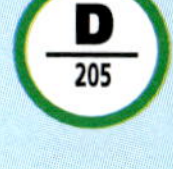

Always drive in accordance with the conditions. Your stopping distance will be affected by
* your speed
* the condition of the road (in wet weather double your separation distance)
* the condition of your tyres.

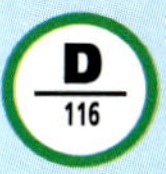

Traffic calming and road surfaces

Traffic calming is used to slow down traffic and make the roads safer for vulnerable road users, especially pedestrians. One of the most common measures are road humps (sometimes called speed humps). Stay within the speed limit and don't overtake other vehicles within these areas.

"ONE OF THE MOST COMMON MEASURES ARE SPEED HUMPS"

In towns where trams operate, the areas used by the trams may have a different surface texture or colour. This may be edged with white line markings.

Rumble bars (raised markings across the road) are often used in rural areas to

- alert you to a hazard, such as a roundabout
- encourage you to reduce speed.

"RUMBLE BARS (RAISED MARKINGS ACROSS THE ROAD) ARE OFTEN USED IN RURAL AREAS TO ALERT YOU TO A HAZARD"

FAQs

Do I need to leave sidelights on when I park on a two-way road?

Leave your sidelights on
- if the speed limit's more than 30 mph
- when it's foggy.

Always park on the left.

I'm following a slow-moving vehicle. I want to overtake but it's been signalling right for some time. What should I do?

Wait for the signal to be cancelled before overtaking. The other driver may have misjudged the distance to a road junction or there might be a hidden hazard.

Are there any times when I can overtake on the left?

Yes

- *if you're in a one-way street*
- *when the vehicle in front is signalling to turn right*
- *in slow-moving queues when traffic in the right-hand lane is moving more slowly than traffic in your lane.*

Am I allowed to wait in a box junction?

Yes, if you want to turn right and your exit's clear but you're prevented from turning by oncoming traffic.

9 Motorway rules

Motorways are designed to help traffic travel faster. Conditions change more quickly so you need to be especially alert at all times.

Check your vehicle thoroughly before starting a long motorway journey. Continuous high speeds may increase the risk of your vehicle breaking down.

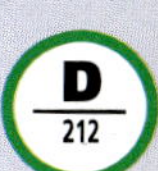

Driving on the motorway

To join the motorway

- use the slip road to adjust your speed to traffic already on the motorway
- always give way to traffic already on the motorway.

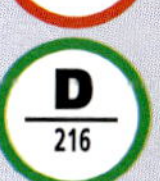

Once you've joined the motorway, keep in the left-hand lane while you get used to the higher speeds of motorway traffic.

All traffic should normally use the left-hand lane of the motorway unless overtaking, regardless of the speed they're travelling. Use the middle and right-hand lane only for overtaking other vehicles.

When you overtake

- normally only overtake on the right
- you may overtake on the left if traffic is moving slowly in queues and the queue on your right is moving more slowly than the one you're in.

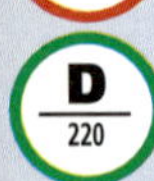

Where there's a steep uphill gradient, a separate crawler lane may be provided for slow-moving vehicles. This helps the faster-moving traffic to flow more easily.

If you're travelling in the left-hand lane and traffic is joining from a slip road, move to another lane if you're able. This helps the flow of traffic joining the motorway, especially at peak times.

Countdown markers on the left-hand verge indicate that you're approaching the next exit. If you want to leave the motorway, try to get into the left-hand lane in good time. If, by mistake, you go past the exit you wanted, carry on to the next one. Never try to stop or reverse.

Speed limits

The national speed limit for cars and motorcycles on a motorway is 70 mph. The same limit applies to all lanes. Obey any signs showing a lower speed limit.

A vehicle towing a trailer
- is restricted to a lower speed limit of 60 mph
- is not allowed to travel in the right-hand lane of a three-lane motorway unless there are lane closures.

You can use your hazard lights to show following traffic that the traffic ahead is slowing down or stopping suddenly. Switch them off as soon as a queue forms behind you.

As you approach any roadworks, take extra care. There are usually lower speed limits,

especially if there's a contraflow system.
- Obey all speed limits.
- Keep a good distance from the vehicle ahead.

HC
263-4

D
232

"REFLECTIVE STUDS HELP YOU TO IDENTIFY YOUR POSITION ON THE CARRIAGEWAY"

Lane markings

HC
111

D
231

Reflective studs help you to identify your position on the carriageway, especially at night or in fog. The different colours are as follows:
- red – between the hard shoulder and carriageway
- amber – between the edge of the carriageway and the central reservation
- white – between lanes
- green – between the carriageway and slip roads
- green/yellow – at contraflow systems and roadworks.

Stopping and breakdowns

Only stop on the motorway
- if flashing red lights show above every lane
- when told to do so by the police
- in a traffic jam
- in an emergency or breakdown.

Move over if signals on the overhead gantries advise you to do so.

Only stop on the hard shoulder in an emergency. To stop for any other reason, such as to have a rest or look at a map, either leave at the next exit or go to a service area.

If your vehicle breaks down or has a puncture, try to get onto the hard shoulder and call for help. If you can, use one of the emergency telephones which are

* normally at one mile intervals. Marker posts at 100 metre intervals point you in the direction of the nearest phone
* connected direct to police control. They will be able to locate you easily.

When using an emergency phone, stand and face oncoming traffic. You can then see any hazards approaching – the draught from a large vehicle could unsteady you if you're taken unawares.

If you decide to use your mobile phone
* check your location (the number on the nearest marker post) before you make the call
* give this information to the emergency services.

To rejoin the carriageway from the hard shoulder, wait for a safe gap and then gain speed on hard shoulder before moving out onto the main carriageway.

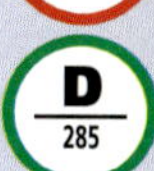

If you're not able to get onto the hard shoulder when you break down

- switch on your hazard warning lights
- leave your vehicle only when you can get clear of the carriageway safely.

FAQs

Can I drive on a motorway with a provisional car or motorcycle licence?

You can't drive on the motorway until you have passed your test, but you can drive on dual carriageways.

"CAN I DRIVE ON A MOTORWAY WITH A PROVISIONAL CAR OR MOTORCYCLE LICENCE?"

I know that pedestrians and horse riders can't use a motorway – what vehicles aren't allowed?

The following vehicles aren't allowed on a motorway:

- *bicycles*
- *motorcycles under 50 cc*
- *most invalid carriages*
- *agricultural vehicles*
- *certain slow-moving vehicles.*

10 Rules of the road

It's important that everyone knows and follows the rules of the road. Some are legal requirements and some are just recommended best practice, but all help to make the roads safer.

Speed limits

You must not exceed the speed limit for the road you're on or your vehicle. Where there isn't any other limit shown, the national speed limit for cars and motorcycles is

- 60 mph on a single carriageway road
- 70 mph on a dual carriageway or motorway.

Lower speed limits of 50 mph and 60 mph respectively apply for vehicles towing a trailer or caravan.

Street lights normally mean that there's a 30 mph speed limit for all vehicles unless signs show otherwise.

On some roads you may also find a minimum speed limit where you should travel above the limit shown on the sign unless it's unsafe to do so.

Always drive with care and according to the conditions. If you're going along a street where cars are parked, keep your speed down and beware of

- pedestrians (especially children) emerging from behind parked vehicles
- vehicles pulling out
- drivers' doors opening.

At roadworks there may be temporary speed limits to slow traffic down. Always obey these signs.

Lanes and junctions

Some roads have lanes reserved for specific vehicles such as cycles, buses or trams. These are marked by signs and road markings, and must only be used by those vehicles during their time of operation.

Never drive or park in a cycle lane marked by a solid white line during its period of operation. Don't drive or park in one marked by a broken line unless it's unavoidable.

Only drive over a footpath to gain access to
a property.

"ONLY DRIVE OVER A FOOTPATH TO GAIN ACCESS TO A PROPERTY"

Treat junctions with extra care. On approach,
move into the appropriate position in good
time. If you're going to turn left, keep well to
the left as you approach the junction.

If you're turning right at a crossroads when an
oncoming driver is also turning right, it's
normally safest to keep the other vehicle to
your right and turn behind it. If you have to
pass in front of the other vehicle, take extra
care as your view may be obscured.

A box junction – indicated by yellow hatched
lines – should be kept clear. Only enter it if your
exit road is clear. You may wait in the box if you
want to turn right and are only prevented from
doing so by oncoming traffic.

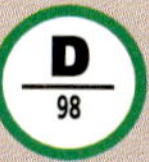

At crossroads where there aren't any signs or
markings, no-one has priority. Check very
carefully in all directions before you proceed.

Roundabouts are designed to aid the flow of traffic. Follow signs and road markings as you approach and negotiate these. Normally, if you're going straight ahead

- don't signal as you approach
- signal left before you leave the roundabout, just after you pass the exit before the one you want.

Some vehicles may not follow the normal rules:

- cyclists and horse riders may stay in the left-hand lane even if they're turning right
- long vehicles may take up a different position to stop the rear of the vehicle hitting the kerb.

Overtaking, turning and reversing

Overtaking is a dangerous manoeuvre. Ask yourself if you really need to overtake and never do so if you're in any doubt as to whether it's safe.

You should normally overtake on the right, but in a one-way street you can overtake on either side. Take extra care if you're overtaking on a dual carriageway, as the right-hand lane can also be used by traffic turning right.

IF YOU'RE ON A BUSY ROAD AND FIND THAT YOU'RE TRAVELLING IN THE WRONG DIRECTION KEEP GOING UNTIL YOU CAN FIND A QUIET SIDE ROAD IN WHICH TO TURN ROUND SAFELY"

If you're on a busy road and find that you're
• travelling in the wrong direction
• in the wrong lane at a busy junction
keep going until you can find somewhere
safe, such as a quiet side road, in which to
turn round.

Never reverse
• for longer than is necessary
• from a side road into a main road.

When reversing into a side road always check
road and traffic conditions in all directions (you
may remove your seat belt while reversing if it
helps you get a better view). If you're not sure
that it's safe, get out and check before you start
to reverse. The greatest hazard to passing traffic
is when the front of your vehicle swings out.

Crossings

If someone is standing on the pavement,
waiting to cross at a zebra crossing, stop, as
long as it's safe to do so, and let them cross.

Pelican crossings are light controlled. When the
red light changes to flashing amber, wait for
any pedestrians to get clear of the crossing
before moving off.

On toucan crossings, cyclists are allowed
to cycle across at the same time as
pedestrians walk.

Level crossings

A level crossing, where a railway line crosses
the road, may have countdown markers to
warn you if the crossing is hidden, such as
round a bend.

- If the warning lights come on as you're approaching the crossing – stop
- If you're already on the crossing when the warning lights come on or a bell rings – keep going and clear the crossing
- If you're waiting at a level crossing, a train has passed but the red lights keep flashing – wait. There may be another train coming.

Stopping and parking

When you park, or leave your vehicle unattended for even the shortest time, always

- switch off the engine
- lock the vehicle
- remove the key.

At night, the safest place to park your vehicle is in your garage, if you have one. If you're away from home try to find a secure car park or park in a well-lit area.

If you have to park on a road, you must leave

"AT NIGHT, THE SAFEST PLACE TO PARK YOUR VEHICLE IS IN A WELL-LIT AREA"

your sidelights on if the speed limit on that road is over 30 mph. Normally park on the left-hand side of the road so other road users can see your reflectors, but in a one-way street you can park on either side.

Never stop on a clearway. On an urban clearway or a road marked with double white lines (even if the one nearest you is broken) you may stop only to set down and pick up passengers.

Don't cause an obstruction by stopping or parking where there are restrictions such as yellow lines and associated signs. In a controlled parking zone you'll have to pay to park. Park within marked bays on the days and times shown on the zone entry signs.

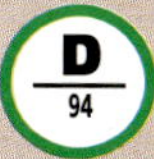

Choose your parking space carefully. Never park illegally or so that you would cause danger or inconvenience to others. Further guidance is given in *The Highway Code*.

FAQs

What do I do if there's an obstruction on my side of the road?

Give way to oncoming traffic if there isn't room for you both to continue safely.

On a dual carriageway, if a sign warns that my lane will close 800 yards ahead, when should I move over?

Move to another lane in good time – don't leave it until the last minute.

"ON A DUAL CARRIAGEWAY, IF A SIGN WARNS THAT MY LANE WILL CLOSE 800 YARDS AHEAD, MOVE TO ANOTHER LANE IN GOOD TIME – DON'T LEAVE IT UNTIL THE LAST MINUTE"

At night, if a car overtakes me, when should I dip my headlights?

Dip your lights as soon as the car passes you or your lights could dazzle the other driver.

I'm on a road that's only wide enough for one vehicle and there's a car coming towards me. What do I do?

Pull into a passing place on your left, or if the nearest passing place is on your right, wait opposite it.

How can brake lights give signals to other drivers?

Brake lights show traffic behind that you're slowing down.

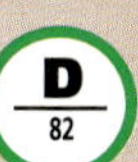

What do I do if I want to turn right onto a dual carriageway that has a narrow central reservation?

Wait until the road is clear in both directions or you'll obstruct traffic coming from your right.

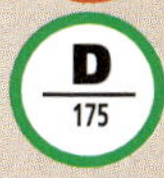

Are there times when I have to stop by law?

Yes. You must stop
- *when involved in an accident*
- *at a red traffic light*
- *when signalled to do so by a police officer or school crossing patrol.*

What different ways can traffic be controlled at roadworks?

Traffic can be controlled by
- *a police officer*
- *traffic lights*
- *a stop-go board.*

In a well-lit built-up area, can I drive using sidelights only?

It's recommended that you use dipped headlights so that you can be seen easily by others.

11 Road and traffic signs

Signs

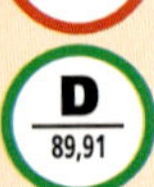

You must comply with all traffic signs and road markings. Road signs can be divided into groups depending on their shape and colour. Each group means something different:

- circular signs give **orders**
  - blue circles give an **instruction**
  - red rings or circles tell you what you **must not do**
- triangular signs give **warnings**
- rectangular signs give **information**.

The exception to the shape rule is the 'STOP' sign – this is octagonal to give it greater prominence and ensure that its meaning is understood even if partly obscured, say by snow.

Maximum speed limit signs are shown by red circles – you must not exceed the speed shown. National speed limits (given on page 67) apply where no specific speed limits are indicated. Speed limit signs may be incorporated in other signs, such as those indicating a traffic-calmed area.

It's impossible to mention all the signs in this small book. *Know Your Traffic Signs* shows all the signs that you're likely to come across. it's important that you familiarise yourself with these so that you don't inadvertently break the law.

Markings on the road give information, orders or warnings. As a general rule, the more paint, the more important the message.

"MARKINGS ON THE ROAD GIVE INFORMATION, ORDERS OR WARNINGS. AS A GENERAL RULE, THE MORE PAINT, THE MORE IMPORTANT THE MESSAGE"

Lines along the road can be divided into

- those along the middle of the road
    - short broken white lines divide lanes
    - longer broken white lines indicate a hazard ahead: only overtake if the road ahead is clear
    - double white lines with a solid white line on your side of the road – you must not cross or straddle the line (see page 82)
    - white diagonal stripes or chevrons – these separate lanes of traffic or protect traffic turning right
- those along the side of the road
    - a white line shows the edge of the carriageway
    - yellow lines show waiting and stopping restrictions
    - zigzag lines (white at pedestrian crossings, yellow outside schools) mean no stopping or parking at any time.

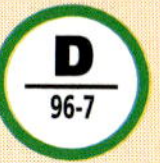

Lines on or across the road
- broken lines across the road mean 'give way' (at a roundabout, give way to traffic from the right)
- solid lines mean 'stop'
- various markings on the road (give way triangles, road hump markings, arrows) warn of a hazard.

As with signs, you should refer to *Know Your Traffic Signs* and *The Highway Code* to get the full picture on road markings.

Reflective studs may be found on motorways and other roads. These are specially useful at night and when visibility is poor (see page 63).

Traffic lights and warning lights
At traffic lights, the sequence of lights and their meaning is
- red – stop and wait at the stop line
- red and amber – stop and wait
- green – go, if the way is clear
- amber – stop unless you've already crossed the stop line or you're so close to it that pulling up might cause an accident
- red (as above).

There may be a green filter arrow. This means that you can go in the direction of the arrow, even if the main light isn't showing green.

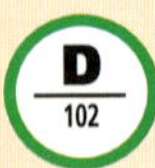

If the traffic lights are out of order, proceed with great care, as nobody has priority. This problem may be brought to your attention by a sign.

You find red flashing lights at level crossings, lifting bridges or outside fire stations. Stop when these show.

"YOU FIND RED FLASHING LIGHTS AT LEVEL CROSSINGS, LIFTING BRIDGES OR OUTSIDE FIRE STATIONS. STOP WHEN THESE SHOW"

On motorways, signals on the overhead gantries or roadside may be accompanied by flashing lights:

- amber – warns you of a hazard (e.g. lane closures, to leave at the next exit, fog) or a temporary maximum speed limit
- red (above your lane) – tells you that the lane is closed beyond this point, so move into another lane
- red (on the central reservation or roadside) – tells you to stop. You must not go beyond that point in any lane.

Signals given by drivers and the police

Drivers normally signal their intention to turn by using their indicators. Ensure that your

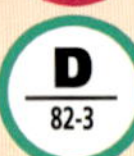

indicators are cancelled after turning to avoid misleading other road users. Be aware that another driver may have left their indicator on by mistake. For example, if you're emerging from a junction and a driver coming along the main road from the right is indicating left, wait until the vehicle starts to turn before you emerge.

An arm signal may be used to strengthen or clarify the message, such as when
- signalling to turn right in busy traffic
- slowing down to give way at a zebra crossing
- slowing down and stopping just after a junction.

Police may signal to you if they're directing traffic.

Ensure you know all arm signals and police signals in case you need to use them.

The horn may be used to warn others of your presence. It must not be used when stationary or between 11.30 pm and 7.00 am, unless another vehicle is likely to cause a danger.

The only reason that you should flash your headlights is to warn other road users that you're there.

A police officer following you in a patrol vehicle may flash their headlights, indicate left and point to the left to get you to stop. Pull up on the left as soon as it's safe to do so.

Use of road lanes

Contraflow lanes are lanes that flow in the opposite direction to the majority of the traffic. Bus and cycle contraflow lanes may be found in one-way streets. They will be signed and marked on the road. Don't enter these lanes.

"CONTRAFLOW LANES MAY BE ENCOUNTERED AT ROADWORKS, WHEN YOU SEE THE SIGNS, REDUCE YOUR SPEED"

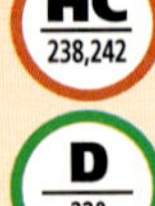

You may also see contraflow lanes at roadworks. When you see the signs, reduce your speed in good time, choose an appropriate lane early and keep the correct separation distance from the vehicle in front.

The right-hand lane of a three-lane motorway is an overtaking lane. Always move back to a lane on your left after overtaking to allow other vehicles to overtake. You may not overtake on your left on a free-flowing motorway or dual carriageway.

FAQs

I've seen some signs with a brown background – does this mean anything in particular?
Signs with a brown background give tourist information.

Sometimes you see lorries with large arrows on the back. What do they mean?
These are placed on slow-moving or stationary maintenance vehicles which are blocking traffic lanes. They show you which side of the vehicle you should pass.

Can I ever cross double white lines where there's a solid white line on my side of the road?
You can cross a solid white line if you're passing a stationary vehicle or overtaking a pedal cycle, horse or road maintenance vehicle, if they're travelling at 10 mph or less.

Can I use my hazard warning lights when I'm moving?
If you're driving on a motorway or unrestricted dual carriageway, you can use your hazard warning lights to warn drivers behind you that there's an obstruction ahead.

82

12 Documents

Before driving on a public road you must have
- a valid tax disc displayed on your vehicle.
  The vehicle registration documents must be
  correct and up to date
- a valid driving licence, which must be signed
- proper insurance cover
- a valid MOT certificate if required.

Licences

The vehicle registration document contains
details of
- the vehicle (including make, model and
  engine size)
- the registered keeper.

HC
p84-5

D
23

You must notify the licensing authority when
you change your vehicle, your name or your
permanent address. If you buy a second-hand
vehicle notify them immediately of the change
of ownership.

A vehicle kept on the public road must have a valid tax disc clearly displayed. This confirms that vehicle excise duty has been paid.

Before driving on a public road, a learner must have a valid provisional driving licence.

You must notify the licensing authority if

• your health is likely to affect your driving
• your eyesight does not meet the required standard.

Insurance

You must have at least third party insurance cover before driving on public roads. This covers
• injury to another person

• damage to someone else's property
• damage to other vehicles.

You'll need to show your insurance certificate when you're taxing your vehicle or if a police officer asks you for it. You may be issued with a temporary cover note until you receive your insurance certificate.

Before you drive anyone else's vehicle, make sure that the vehicle is insured for your use.

The cost of your insurance depends on many factors, but is generally less if you
• are over 25 years old
• complete the Pass Plus scheme.

Your insurance policy may have an excess of a certain amount, say £100. This means that you'll have to pay the first £100 of any claim.

MOT

Cars must have an MOT test when they're three years old (four in Northern Ireland).

Trailers and caravans don't need an MOT, but they do need to be kept in good order.

MOT certificates are valid for one year.

You can drive your car without an MOT certificate when driving to an appointment at an MOT centre.

If your vehicle needs an MOT certificate and you don't have one
• you won't be able to renew your road tax
• it could invalidate your insurance.

FAQs

What happens if the police ask to see my documents and I don't have them with me?
You can produce them at a police station within seven days (five days in Northern Ireland).

"WHAT HAPPENS IF THE POLICE ASK TO SEE MY DOCUMENTS AND I DON'T HAVE THEM WITH ME?" "YOU CAN PRODUCE THEM AT A POLICE STATION WITHIN SEVEN DAYS (FIVE DAYS IN NORTHERN IRELAND)"

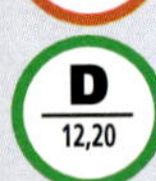

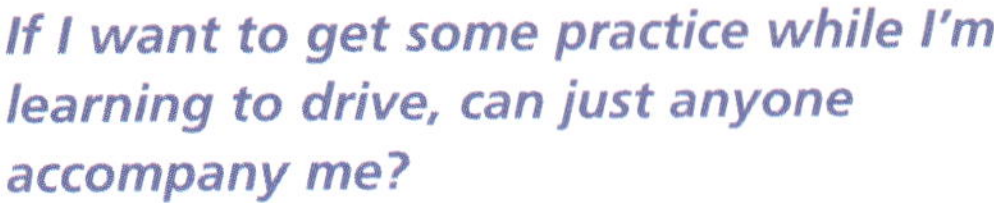

No, the person accompanying you must be 21 years old and have held (and still hold) a full licence for three years.

I've heard that I'm on probation for two years after I've passed my test, what does this mean?

If you get six or more penalty points within two years of passing your practical test, you'll lose your licence. You'll then have to

* reapply for a provisional licence
* retake your theory and practical tests again.

Any points on your provisional licence will be transferred onto your new licence when you pass your test.

13 Accidents

Breakdowns

If a warning light on the instrument panel of your vehicle comes on while you're driving, stop (as soon as you can do so safely) and check out the problem.

If your tyre bursts or you've a puncture while you're driving

- hold the steering wheel firmly
- pull up slowly or roll to a stop at the side of the road.

If this or any other emergency occurs on a motorway, try to get onto the hard shoulder and call for help from the emergency telephones. The police will answer and ask you

- the phone number
- details of yourself and your vehicle
- whether you belong to a motoring organisation.

HC
p90

D
287

HC
244,249

D
284-5

"IF YOUR TYRE BURSTS OR YOU'VE A PUNCTURE WHILE YOU'RE DRIVING ON A MOTORWAY, CALL FOR HELP FROM THE EMERGENCY TELEPHONES"

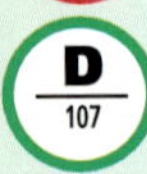

A person who has a disability which affects their mobility may display a HELP pennant if they're unable to reach an emergency phone.

If you break down on a level crossing, get everyone out of the vehicle and clear of the crossing. Then call the signal operator from the phone provided. Only move your vehicle if the operator tells you to do so. If you're waiting at a level crossing and the red light signal continues to flash after a train has gone by, wait, as there may be another train coming.

Warning others of a breakdown or accident

Use your hazard warning lights
- if you need to slow down or stop on a motorway or high-speed road because of an accident or hazard ahead
- when you're broken down or stopped and temporarily obstructing traffic.

If you've a warning triangle, place it at least 45 metres (147 feet) behind your vehicle. This will warn other road users that you've broken down. Never use a warning triangle on a motorway.

Stopping at an accident

If you're the first to arrive at the scene of an accident, stop and warn other traffic. Switch on your hazard warning lights. Don't put yourself at risk:
- make sure the emergency services are called
- switch off the vehicle engine(s)
- move uninjured people away from the scene.

A vehicle carrying dangerous goods will display an orange label or a hazard warning plate on the back. Report what it says when you call the emergency services. The different plates are shown in *The Highway Code*.

First aid

Even if you don't know any first aid, you can help any injured people by

- keeping them warm and comfortable
- keeping them calm by talking to them reassuringly
- making sure that they're not left alone.

"EVEN IF YOU DON'T KNOW ANY FIRST AID, YOU CAN HELP ANY INJURED PEOPLE BY KEEPING THEM WARM AND COMFORTABLE, KEEPING THEM CALM BY TALKING TO THEM REASSURINGLY AND MAKING SURE THAT THEY'RE NOT LEFT ALONE"

Don't move them as long as the area is safe. Only move them if they're in obvious danger,

and then with extreme care. If a motorcyclist is involved, never remove their helmet unless it's essential to keep them alive.

Never offer a casualty a cigarette to calm them down.

If someone is unconscious, follow the 'ABC' code and check their
• **A**irway
• **B**reathing
• **C**irculation (bleeding)

If they're not breathing, consider giving mouth-to-mouth resuscitation:
• check and if necessary clear their mouth and airway
• tilt their head back as far as possible
• pinch their nostrils together.

Only stop when they can breathe without help. If the casualty is a small child, breathe very gently.

If they're bleeding
• apply firm pressure to the wound
• raise the limb as long as it isn't broken.

If someone is suffering from shock
• reassure them constantly
• keep them warm
• loosen any tight clothing
• make sure they're not left alone.

If someone is suffering from burns
• douse the burns thoroughly with cool liquid
• don't remove anything sticking to the burn.

Reporting

If you're involved in an accident, stop. It's an offence not to stop and call the police if any other person is injured or there's damage to another vehicle, property or animal.

If another vehicle is involved, find out
- whether the other driver owns the vehicle
- the make and registration number of the vehicle
- the other driver's name, address and telephone number and details of their insurance.

The police may ask you to produce, following an accident (or at any other time)
- your insurance certificate
- the MOT certificate for the vehicle you're driving
- your driving licence.

FAQs

What should I do if I see something fall from a lorry on the motorway?

Stop at the next emergency telephone and report it to the police. Do the same if anything falls from your own vehicle – don't try to retrieve it yourself.

What would you suggest I carry in my car for use in an emergency?

It's useful to have a first aid kit, a warning triangle and a fire extinguisher. This equipment could be invaluable and is a small price to pay if it helps to prevent or lessen an injury.

What should I do if I smell petrol?

Stop and investigate as soon as you can do so safely. Don't ignore it. It can be useful to carry a fire extinguisher, which may help in tackling a small fire, but don't take any risks.

14 Vehicle loading

Vehicle stability

You, as a driver, are responsible for making sure that your vehicle isn't overloaded. Overloading can seriously affect the handling, especially steering.

Securely fasten any load carried on a roof rack. A heavy load will reduce the stability of your vehicle.

Passengers

All passengers should wear seat belts if they're fitted. You, as a driver, are responsible for ensuring that all children (under 14 years) wear a suitable restraint. The type of restraint varies with the age of the child. For example, for a child under 3 years one of the following is suitable:

- a baby carrier
- a harness
- a child seat.

Under no circumstances should a passenger travel in a caravan while it's being towed.

Towing

If you're planning to tow a caravan, it'll help the handling of your vehicle if you have a stabiliser fitted to your towbar. You can also fit a breakaway cable to the trailer braking system as an additional safety device.

If a trailer or caravan starts to swerve or snake as you're driving along, ease off the accelerator and reduce your speed gradually to regain control.

On a three-lane motorway, towing vehicles are restricted to

- a 60 mph speed limit
- the left-hand and centre lanes only – they must not use the right-hand lane.

FAQs

I know that as a driver I'm responsible for ensuring all children in my car use a suitable restraint. Is there anything else I can do to protect them?

Child safety door locks are worth considering. These prevent children opening the rear doors themselves.

Should my tyres always be inflated to the same pressure?

Inflate your tyres to a higher pressure

- *when you're carrying a heavy load*
- *if you're driving fast for a long distance, such as on a motorway.*

Your vehicle handbook should tell you the correct pressure for different circumstances.

Question paper

Answers may be found at the rear
of this section

Question 1

You have to leave valuables in your car. It would
be safer to (*Mark one answer*)

- [ ] put them in a carrier bag
- [ ] park near a school entrance
- [ ] lock them out of sight
- [ ] park near a bus stop

Question 2

You are driving in very wet weather. Your
vehicle begins to slide. This effect is called
(*Mark one answer*)

- [ ] hosing
- [ ] weaving
- [ ] aquaplaning
- [ ] fading

Question 3

Which sign means that pedestrians may be
walking along the road? (*Mark one answer*)

- [ ] 
- [ ] 
- [ ] 
- [ ] 

Question 4

You see a car on the hard shoulder of a
motorway with a HELP pennant displayed.
This means the driver is most likely to be
(Mark one answer)

- [ ] a disabled person
- [ ] first aid trained
- [ ] a foreign visitor
- [ ] a rescue patrol person

Question 5

You start to feel tired while driving.
What should you do? *(Mark one answer)*

- [ ] Increase your speed slightly
- [ ] Decrease your speed slightly
- [ ] Find a less busy route
- [ ] Pull over at a safe place to rest

Question 6

You are intending to turn right at a crossroads.
An oncoming driver is also turning right. It will
normally be safer to *(Mark one answer)*

- [ ] keep the other vehicle to your RIGHT
  and turn behind it (offside to offside)

- [ ] keep the other vehicle to your LEFT and
  turn in front of it (nearside to nearside)

- [ ] carry on and turn at the next junction
  instead

- [ ] hold back and wait for the other driver
  to turn first

Question 7

While driving, you approach roadworks.
You see a temporary maximum speed limit sign.
You must *(Mark one answer)*

☐ comply with the sign during the
working day

☐ comply with the sign at all times

☐ comply with the sign when the lanes
are narrow

☐ comply with the sign during the hours
of darkness

Question 8

Which FOUR of these must NOT use
motorways? *(Mark four answers)*

☐ Learner car drivers
☐ Motorcycles over 50cc
☐ Double-decker buses
☐ Farm tractors
☐ Learner motorcyclists
☐ Cyclists

Question 9

You are approaching a pelican crossing. The
amber light is flashing. You must
(Mark one answer)

☐ give way to pedestrians who are crossing
☐ encourage pedestrians to cross
☐ not move until the green light appears
☐ stop even if the crossing is clear

Question 10

You are following other vehicles in fog with your lights on. How else can you reduce the chances of being involved in an accident? *(Mark one answer)*

☐ Keep close to the vehicle in front

☐ Use your main beam instead of dipped headlights

☐ Keep together with the faster vehicles

☐ Reduce your speed and increase the gap

Question 11

When going through a contraflow system on a motorway you should *(Mark one answer)*

☐ ensure that you do not exceed 30 mph

☐ keep a good distance from the vehicle ahead

☐ switch lanes to keep the traffic flowing

☐ stay close to the vehicle ahead to reduce queues

Question 12

You think the driver of the vehicle in front has forgotten to cancel the right indicator. You should *(Mark one answer)*

☐ flash your lights to alert the driver

☐ sound your horn before overtaking

☐ overtake on the left if there is room

☐ stay behind and not overtake

Question 13

You arrive at an accident where someone is
suffering from severe burns. You should
(Mark one answer)

☐ burst any blisters

☐ douse the burns thoroughly with cool
liquid

☐ apply lotions to the injury

☐ remove anything sticking to the burns

Question 14

You are travelling along a
motorway. You see this sign.
You should *(Mark one answer)*

☐ leave the motorway at the next exit
☐ turn left immediately
☐ change lane
☐ move onto the hard shoulder

Question 15

You are following a cyclist.
You wish to turn left just
ahead. You should
(Mark one answer)

☐ overtake the cyclist before the junction

☐ pull alongside the cyclist and stay level
until after the junction

☐ hold back until the cyclist has passed the
junction

☐ go around the cyclist on the junction

Question 16

Which of these signs means that the national speed limit applies? *(Mark one answer)*

Question 17

Which of the following types of glasses should NOT be worn when driving at night?
(Mark one answer)

☐ Half-moon

☐ Round

☐ Bi-focal

☐ Tinted

Question 18

When leaving your vehicle where should you park if possible? *(Mark one answer)*

☐ Opposite a traffic island

☐ In a secure car park

☐ On a bend

☐ At or near a taxi rank

Question 19

You are turning left at a
junction. Pedestrians have
started to cross the road.
You should *(Mark one answer)*

- [ ] go on, giving them plenty of room
- [ ] stop and wave at them to cross
- [ ] blow your horn and proceed
- [ ] give way to them

Question 20

How would you react to drivers who appear to
be inexperienced? *(Mark one answer)*

- [ ] Sound your horn to warn them of your
  presence

- [ ] Be patient and prepare for them to react
  more slowly

- [ ] Flash your headlights to indicate that it is
  safe for them to proceed

- [ ] Overtake them as soon as possible

Question 21

What does this sign mean?
(Mark one answer)

- [ ] No motor vehicles
- [ ] End of motorway
- [ ] No through road
- [ ] End of bus lane

Question 22

You have just passed these warning lights. What hazard would you expect to see next? *(Mark one answer)*

- [ ] A level crossing with no barrier
- [ ] An ambulance station
- [ ] A school crossing patrol
- [ ] An opening bridge

Question 23

Your vehicle has anti-lock brakes, but they may not always prevent skidding. This is most likely to happen when driving *(Mark two answers)*

- [ ] in foggy conditions
- [ ] on surface water
- [ ] on loose road surfaces
- [ ] on dry tarmac
- [ ] at night on unlit roads

Question 24

A properly adjusted head restraint will *(Mark one answer)*

- [ ] make you more comfortable
- [ ] help you to avoid neck injury
- [ ] help you to relax
- [ ] help you to maintain your driving position

Question 25
A vehicle pulls out in front of you at a junction.
What should you do? *(Mark one answer)*

☐ Swerve past it and sound your horn

☐ Flash your headlights and drive up close
behind

☐ Slow down and be ready to stop

☐ Accelerate past it immediately

Question 26
A newly qualified driver must
(Mark one answer)

☐ display green 'L' plates

☐ not exceed 40 mph for 12 months

☐ be accompanied on a motorway

☐ have valid motor insurance

Question 27
You are approaching traffic lights that have
been on green for some time. You should
(Mark one answer)

☐ accelerate hard

☐ maintain your speed

☐ be ready to stop

☐ brake hard

Question 28

You are trying to move off on snow. You should use *(Mark one answer)*

☐ the lowest gear you can

☐ the highest gear you can

☐ a high engine speed

☐ the handbrake and footbrake together

Question 29

On a motorway this sign means
(Mark one answer)

☐ move over onto the hard shoulder

☐ overtaking on the left only

☐ leave the motorway at the next exit

☐ move to the lane on your left

Question 30

Which sign means 'no entry'?
(Mark one answer)

☐

☐

☐

☐

Question 31

The road is wet. Why might a motorcyclist steer round drain covers on a bend?
(Mark one answer)

☐ To avoid puncturing the tyres on the edge of the drain covers

☐ To prevent the motorcycle sliding on the metal drain covers

☐ To help judge the bend using the drain covers as marker points

☐ To avoid splashing pedestrians on the pavement

Question 32

For which TWO of these may you use hazard warning lights? *(Mark two answers)*

☐ When driving on a motorway to warn drivers behind of a hazard ahead

☐ When you are double parked on a two way road

☐ When your direction indicators are not working

☐ When warning oncoming traffic that you intend to stop

☐ When your vehicle has broken down and is causing an obstruction

Question 33

In daylight, an approaching motorcyclist is using a dipped headlight. Why? *(Mark one answer)*

☐ So that the rider can be seen more easily

☐ To stop the battery overcharging

☐ To improve the rider's vision

☐ The rider is inviting you to proceed

Question 34

You are driving along this road. What should you be prepared to do?
(Mark one answer)

☐ Sound your horn and continue

☐ Slow down and give way

☐ Report the driver to the police

☐ Squeeze through the gap

Question 35

Overloading your vehicle can seriously affect the *(Mark two answers)*

☐ gearbox

☐ steering

☐ handling

☐ battery life

☐ journey time

Answers

Question 1 *Lock them out of sight*
Question 2 *Aquaplaning*

Question 3 

Question 4 *A disabled person*
Question 5 *Pull over at a safe place to rest*
Question 6 *Keep the other vehicle on your RIGHT and turn behind it (offside to offside)*
Question 7 *Comply with the sign at all times*
Question 8 *Learner car drivers, Farm tractors, Learner motorcyclists, Cyclists*
Question 9 *Give way to pedestrians who are crossing*
Question 10 *Reduce your speed and increase the gap*
Question 11 *Keep a good distance from the vehicle ahead*
Question 12 *Stay behind and not overtake*
Question 13 *Douse the burns thoroughly with cool liquid*
Question 14 *Leave the motorway at the next exit*
Question 15 *Hold back until the cyclist has passed the junction*

Question 16 

Question 17 *Tinted*
Question 18 *In a secure car park*
Question 19 *Give way to them*
Question 20 *Be patient and prepare for them to react more slowly*
Question 21 *End of motorway*
Question 22 *A school crossing patrol*

Question 23 *On surface water, on loose road surfaces*

Question 24 *Help you to avoid neck injury*

Question 25 *Slow down and be ready to stop*

Question 26 *Have valid motor insurance*

Question 27 *Be ready to stop*

Question 28 *The highest gear you can*

Question 29 *Move to the lane on your left*

Question 30 

Question 31 *To prevent the motorcycle sliding on the metal drain covers*

Question 32 *When driving on a motorway to warn drivers behind of a hazard ahead, When your vehicle has broken down and is causing an obstruction*

Question 33 *So that the rider can be seen more easily*

Question 34 *Slow down and give way*

Question 35 *Steering, handling*

Notes

Notes